People of the Bible

The Bible through stories and pictures

The
First Easter

Copyright © in this format Belitha Press Ltd., 1984

Text copyright © Catherine Storr 1984

Illustrations copyright © Chris Molan 1984

Art Director: Treld Bicknell

First published in the United States of America 1984
by Raintree Publishers Inc.
310 West Wisconsin Avenue, Milwaukee, Wisconsin 53203
in association with Belitha Press Ltd., London.

Conceived, designed and produced by Belitha Press Ltd.,
2 Beresford Terrace, London N5 2DH

ISBN 0-8172-1987-0 (U.S.A.)

Library of Congress Cataloging in Publication Data

Storr, Catherine.
    The first Easter.

    (People of the Bible)
    Summary: Retells the story of the death and
resurrection of Jesus.
        1. Jesus Christ—Resurrection—Juvenile literature.
2. Jesus Christ—Crucifixion—Juvenile literature.
[1. Jesus Christ—Crucifixion. 2. Jesus Christ—
Resurrection. 3. Easter. 4. Bible stories—N.T.]
I. Molan, Christine, ill. II. Title.
BT481.S85   1983   232.9′6   83-13917

ISBN 0-8172-1987-0

    5 6 7 8 9 10 11 12 13 14   98 97 96 95 94 93 92 91 90 89

The First Easter

Retold by Catherine Storr

Pictures by Chris Molan

Raintree Childrens Books
Milwaukee
Belitha Press Limited • London

It was the time of the Passover.
Jesus knew that he was coming to the
end of his work in this world. He told
his disciples Peter and John to go into
Jerusalem, where they would meet a
man carrying a pitcher of water.

When they found him, they asked if
Jesus and his disciples could celebrate
the Passover in his upstairs guest
room.

While they were eating the Passover supper in the upper room, Jesus said, "One of you is going to betray me to my enemies—the high priests and the Roman governor of the city."

Each disciple asked, "Is it me? Is it me?"
Jesus said, "It will be the one who dips his
hand into the dish with me." Jesus took bread
and broke it. Then he gave his disciples wine.
He said, "Eat this bread and drink this wine in
remembrance of me."

After they had sung a hymn, they all went out to the Mount of Olives. Jesus told the disciples, "Tonight you will all be in trouble because of me."

Peter said, "Everyone else may be in trouble, but I will always stand by you." But Jesus said, "Before the cock crows tomorrow morning, you will three times deny that you know me."

Jesus left his disciples in the Garden of Gethsemane and went up the mountain to pray. He was very sorrowful. Three times he came back to see his disciples, but each time they were asleep. Jesus said, "Couldn't you watch with me for one hour?" But he knew that they were very tired.

Then he said, "It is time we left here. The crowds and the disciple who is going to betray me are coming."

It was Judas Iscariot who gave Jesus away to the high priests and the elders. They paid him thirty pieces of silver to tell them where Jesus was. Judas said to them, "The man I shall greet with a kiss is the man you want."

When Judas saw Jesus, he said, "Hail Master" and kissed him. At once, the people caught hold of Jesus and took him prisoner.

When Peter saw this, he was angry and he drew his sword. He cut off one man's ear. But Jesus said, "Put up your sword. I don't need it. My father in heaven could send twelve legions of angels if I wanted to be kept safe." Then he healed the man's ear.

The crowd took Jesus to the house of Caiaphas, the High Priest. Many people came there to swear that Jesus had pretended to be the King of the Jews. They said he had plotted against the Romans who ruled the country.

While this was going on, Peter was outside. A girl came up to him and said, "You are a friend of that Jesus." Peter said, "No, I don't know him." Then two more people said, "You were with Jesus of Nazareth." Peter also told them that he didn't know Jesus.

Then suddenly the cock crowed. Peter remembered what Jesus had told him. He went outside and wept bitterly.

In the morning, the high priests and elders took Jesus to Pontius Pilate, the Roman governor, to have him condemned to death. When Judas saw this, he tried to give back the thirty pieces of silver to the high priests. But they would not take them. Judas felt very bad because he knew that Jesus had done nothing wrong. Judas felt so guilty that he went and hanged himself.

When Pontius Pilate saw Jesus, he asked, "Are you the King of the Jews?"

Jesus said, "Those are your words, not mine."

Pilate asked him a great many questions, but he could not find anything that Jesus had done wrong. Pilate said to the people, "This man is innocent. Shall I let him go?" But the people cried, "No! Release Barabbas, the robber, instead."

While Pilate was wondering what to do, his wife sent him a message. She said, "Don't let this good man be killed. I had a dream about him last night." But Pilate knew that the crowds of people wanted him to set Barabbas free, not Jesus. Pilate was afraid to go against the crowd. So he washed his hands in front of them and said, "I am innocent of the blood of this good man."

Before the soldiers took Jesus outside the city to be killed, they mocked Jesus. They put a crown of thorns on his head and gave him a purple robe. Then they pretended to worship him. They whipped him and made him carry a wooden cross to Calvary, the place where he was to be crucified.

Jesus was crucified between two thieves. The soldiers taunted him. They said, "If you are the son of God, get down off your cross." But Jesus prayed to God, "Father, forgive them, they don't know what they are doing."

After three hours in the hot sun, Jesus died.

A man called Joseph of Arimathea came to put Jesus' body in a tomb. He wrapped Jesus' body in linen and spices, and rolled an enormous stone in front of the tomb to keep the body safe. Early the next morning, Mary Magdalene went to the tomb and found it empty. The stone had been rolled away.

Mary saw a figure in a long white robe sitting in the tomb. The figure asked her, "Why do you cry?" Mary said, "Because they have taken away the body."

Mary went out into the garden and saw someone whom she thought must be a gardener. She asked him, "Please, do you know what happened to Jesus' body?" Then he said, "Mary!"

She looked and saw that it was Jesus. He had come back from the dead.

She said, "Master!" and was filled with joy.

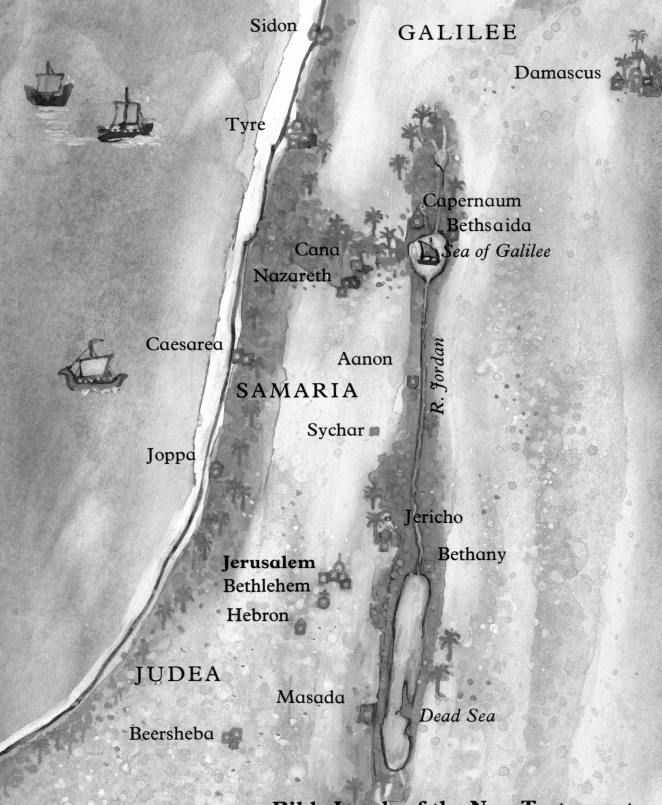

Sidon

GALILEE

Damascus

Tyre

Capernaum
Bethsaida
Sea of Galilee

Cana
Nazareth

Caesarea

Aanon

SAMARIA

R. Jordan

Sychar

Joppa

Jericho
Bethany

Jerusalem
Bethlehem
Hebron

JUDEA

Masada

Dead Sea

Beersheba

Bible Lands of the New Testament